passport prayers

to: ....

from: ....

date: ....

#PassportPrayersJournal

 @NewHopeRBC + @NotYoGrandMaMasBibleStudy

 @NewHopeRBC + @NotYoGrandMaMasBibleStudy

 www.NewHopeRBC.com

passport prayers TRAVEL JOURNAL FOR GLOBAL ADVENTURES

Copyright © 2025 by D Nicole Williams

All rights reserved.

No portion of this publication may be reproduced, distributed, or transmitted in any form or by any means, including photocopying, recording, or other electronic or mechanical methods, without the prior written permission of the publisher, except in the case of brief quotations embodied in critical reviews and certain other noncommercial uses permitted by copyright law.

For permission requests, email the publisher, addressed "ATTN: Permissions" at the following: NewHope@NewHopeRBC.com

Bulk discounts are available on quantity purchases by associations, corporations, and others for business, educational and ministry use. For details, contact the publisher at the address above.

ISBN: 978-1-942650-57-7

WHERE TO
WHERE
WHERE TO
HERE TO
WHERE TO
WHERE TO
WHERE
WHERE
WHER
WH
WH
WHERE
WHERE TO
WHERE TO
WHERE
WHERE TO

FIVE
PRAYERS FOR

A FEW OF MY
favorite places

ISRAEL
SYDNEY
ARUBA

take a peek at my *travel* vision

PRAYERS

where to ???

A FEW OF MY

enjoy the trip

Who am I taking with me on my next trip?

> *What countries would you like to visit?*

PRAY FOR THOSE PLACES

What are my prayers regarding traveling business class?

news flash

pray now!

must see travel destinations

pray now
pray now
pray now
pray now
pray now
pray now
pray now
pray now
pray now

WHAT LANGUAGES WILL YOU LEARN TO SPEAK?

pray now!

What was your worst trip?

WHAT IS THE MOST INTERESTING CITY TO VISIT IN YOUR COUNTRY?

PRAY FOR THAT CITY

Pray about overcoming difficult situations while traveling.

_____

_____

IF YOU TRAVELED TO EUROPE,
   WHAT COUNTRIES WOULD LIKE TO VISIT?

pray now!

WHERE TO
WHERE
WHERE TO
WHERE TO
WHERE TO
WHERE TO
WHERE
WHERE TO
WHERE TO
WHERE
WHERE TO
WHERE TO
WHERE TO
WHERE
WHERE TO

41

FAVORITE BUDGET FRIENDLY RESORTS

pray now
pray now
pray now
pray now
pray now
pray now
pray now
pray now
pray now
pray now

Have you ever gotten lost while traveling?

WHY DO YOU TRAVEL?

3
prayers
for travel
with
KIDS
pray now!

Life is either
a daring adventure
or nothing.

> When traveling with someone,
> take large doses of patience
> and tolerance with your morning coffee.
> – Helen Hayes

HOW MANY TIMES HAVE YOU BEEN ON AN AIRPLANE?

MY FAVORITE THING TO DO IS

**GO WHERE
I'VE NEVER BEEN**

Fill your life with experiences, **NOT THINGS.**

Have stories to tell, **NOT STUFF TO SHOW.**

travel prayers

Lets get lost

**YOU'LL MISS
THE BEST THINGS**
if you keep your eyes shut

DREAM HIGHER THAN THE SKY AND DEEPER THAN THE OCEAN

pray now

★★★★★

**EVERY EXIT
IS AN ENTRY
SOMEWHERE
ELSE**

exploration
destinations

NOTIFICATION

Life is meant for exploring

yes   *absolutely*

PEOPLE FORGET YEARS
AND *remember moments*

Journey with God in Prayer

5 PRAYERS for getting the best travel deals

pray now, travel more

7 PRAYERS

CARRY AS LITTLE AS POSSIBLE, BUT *choose that little with care.*

— Earl Shaffer

The more I traveled the more I realized that fear makes strangers of people who should be friends.

— *Shirley MacLaine*

> TO AWAKEN ALONE IN **A STRANGE TOWN** IS ONE OF THE PLEASANTEST SENSATIONS IN THE WORLD.
> – Freya Stark

What is the ideal length for a vacation?

THERE ARE NO FOREIGN LANDS.

IT IS THE TRAVELER ONLY WHO IS FOREIGN.

ONCE A YEAR

GO SOMEPLACE YOU'VE NEVER BEEN BEFORE

The farther you go, however, the **harder it is to return.** The world has many edges, and it's easy to fall off.

ANDERSON COOPER

IN THE END,
WE ONLY REGRET
THE CHANCES WE DIDN'T TAKE.

#PassportPrayersJournal

:camera: @NewHopeRBC + @NotYoGrandMaMasBibleStudy
:facebook: @NewHopeRBC + @NotYoGrandMaMasBibleStudy
:cursor: www.NewHopeRBC.com

www.ingramcontent.com/pod-product-compliance
Lightning Source LLC
Chambersburg PA
CBHW041915230426
43673CB00016B/410